Bibliografische Information der Deutschen Nationalbibliothek:

Die Deutsche Bibliothek verzeichnet diese Publikation in der Deutschen National-bibliografie; detaillierte bibliografische Daten sind im Internet über http://dnb.d-nb.de/ abrufbar.

Impressum:

Copyright © 2009 GRIN Verlag
Druck und Bindung: Books on Demand GmbH, Norderstedt Germany
ISBN: 9783668706620

Dieses Buch bei GRIN:

https://www.grin.com/document/129351

Alena Angelovicova

Purposes and Principles of the UN

GRIN Verlag

GRIN - Your knowledge has value

Der GRIN Verlag publiziert seit 1998 wissenschaftliche Arbeiten von Studenten, Hochschullehrern und anderen Akademikern als eBook und gedrucktes Buch. Die Verlagswebsite www.grin.com ist die ideale Plattform zur Veröffentlichung von Hausarbeiten, Abschlussarbeiten, wissenschaftlichen Aufsätzen, Dissertationen und Fachbüchern.

Besuchen Sie uns im Internet:

http://www.grin.com/

http://www.facebook.com/grincom

http://www.twitter.com/grin_com

The scope of the essay

The aim of this essay is to outline and examine the purposes and the principles of the United Nations Organisation (hereinafter the UN) and assess the effectiveness of its principal organs. The idea of the UN as a successor of League of Nations (hereinafter LN) was presented during the Second World War. The failure of LN, presented by the outbreak of Second World War, was the main impulse to create the international organisation capable of ensuring international peace and cooperation between all states of the international community.

The purposes of the UN

Maintaining of the international peace and security[1] (Art.1 para1) evolves as first and main of the purposes of the UN. Developing friendly relations among nations (Art.1 para 2) and attaining international co-operation in solving international problems and promoting the respect for human rights and fundamental freedoms[2] (Art.1 para.3) appear as means of securing the international peace and security but as purposes on its own, too.

The UN organs exercise their competences through the provisions of the UN Charter in order to maintain the international peace and security, namely through the provisions necessary to prevent the occurrence of the situation which might lead to the threat to the peace or breach of the peace (the General Assembly's [hereinafter the GA] competence to discuss and make an recommendation on any question within the UN Charter under Art.10 and Art.11), or if there is a situation endangering the peace, through the provisions of the peaceful settlement of the dispute (the GA and the Security Council [hereinafter the SC] act under Chapter VI), or if there is threat to the peace or breach to the peace or act of aggression (the SC acts under Chapter VII). The provision of Art.1 para 4 stresses out the importance of the consensus of the member states as prerequisite in the achieving the purposes mentioned above.

---

[1] The UN organs, particularly the GA, refers to the principles and purposes of the UN in the decisions, e.g. The UNGA Res. 377 (V) (3 November 1950).
[2] The UNGA Res. 820 9IX (14 December 1954) invoked the Art.1para 3 "protection of human rights" in

The principles of the UN

The principles of the UN, as they are stated in Art. 2 set forth the obligations for the member states or the organisation itself and need to be put in context with purposes of the UN.

The principle of self-determination

The principle evolves from Art.1 para 2 and refers to a mean to ensure the international peace and security. The UN Charter nor gives the definition of the principle, neither determines the way of its realization. The realization of the principle can be seen in the process of de-colonisation which is undoubtly considered the success of the UN. The provision of the UN Charter (Art.73) imposed to the colonial empires the obligation to promote political, educational, social development of the non-self-governing territories without necessity to grant the independence. It was not until the GA adopted the Declaration on the granting of independence to colonial countries and peoples, that submission to the colonial empire was to be considered non conformed with the UN Charter.[3] Declaration on principles of international law concerning friendly relations and co-operation among states in accordance with the UN Charter (hereinafter the Declaration on Friendly Relations) further restated the principle by endorsing the end of the colonialism.[4] Apart from the de-colonisation, the application of the principle (external self-determination) can be seen in reaffirming the independence to the people under foreign occupation and also to racial groups without the representative government.[5] The principle has become the part of customary international rule as consequence of the UN practice, however, its realization has to be restricted. As Cassese points out, the principle of self-determination cannot be applied without its limits, as such, it cannot be the foundation of demands of the ethnic groups, or religious, and cultural minorities.[6] His view is the reflection of the correlation between

---

the context of the question of racial conflict in South Africa deriving from the policy of apartheid.

[3] The UNGA Res. 1514 (14 December 1960) in the process of de-colonisation the GA played the significant role which certainly can be even more supported by the binding character of the decisions covering the measures to ensure the independence of non-self-governing territories.

[4] The UNGA Res. 2625 (XXV) (24 October 1970).

[5] The UNGA Res. 39/13 (15 November 1984) reaffirming the right of self-determination to the Afghanistan people under the occupation of Soviet Union.

[6] Antonio Cassese, *International Law*, (second edition, Oxford University Press, Oxford, 2005) 60-68.

the principle of self-determination and its application leading to secession on the one hand, and the principle of sovereignty, on the other one.[7]

The principle of sovereign equality of the states

Having said that the UN Charter is state centrilised document, the principle of sovereign equality of the states Art.2 para1 emerges as the first one. The principle covers two conceptions (sovereignty and equality). "The principle of sovereignty[8] of the state includes the following elements:

a) juridical equality;

b) exercising the rights in full sovereignty;

c) duty to respect the personality of other states;

d) inviolability of the territorial integrity and political independence;

e) the right freely to choose political, social system ;

f) the duty to comply fully and in good faith with international obligations and to live in peace with other states ."[9]

The limitation of the sovereignty of the state deriving from its membership to the UN is based on the agreement and thus it doesn't infringe the principle itself, which is furthermore stated in Art.2 para 7 non-intervention of the UN in domestic jurisdiction of the state. Furthermore Art. 2 para 4, the prohibition of use of force, is not considered the limitation of the sovereignty, but rather the requirement for its full application. The principle of equality, as second element of the principle, indicates the equality of the states before the law disregarding the size of the state.[10]

---

[7] Bearing in mind the character of the UN Charter as state centrilised document, the realization of the right of self-determination cannot override the principle of sovereignty in such way that it could lead to the fragmentation of international community. In this view, the self-determination is rather need for the protection of human rights than the right of the groups of people for the separation from the state that they belong to. The UNGA Res. 2625 (24 October 1970), the Declaration on Friendly Relations, in defence of the previous statement proclaims that by exercising the right of self-determination nothing will authorise or encourage any action which will intervene the territorial integrity of sovereign state or secession providing that government observes the principle of self-determination and it represents the whole population of the territory regardless of race, religion, or colour.

[8] In its judgment from Corfu Channel Case the ICJ has determined the violation of the principle of sovereignty of Albania by the UK, *Corfu Channel Case (UK v Albania)* (Merits) [1949] ICJ Rep 4.

[9] The UNGA Res. 2625 (XXV) (24 October 1970), the Declaration on Friendly Relations .

[10] In reality it covers a different set of rights and obligations as it can be seen from the position of permanent members of the SC and their power of veto.

The principle of the duty of the member states to fulfill in good faith the obligations in accordance with the UN Charter.

The principle, arising from Art.2 para 2, is nothing more than the declaration of the customary rule *pacta sunt servanda.*[11]

The principle of settling the international dispute by peaceful means

The principle, arising, from Art.2 para.3, obligates member states to settle international disputes by peaceful means. The application of the principle, specified furthermore by the Chapter VI of the UN Charter, despite the broad power of the GA and the SC, depends thus on will of the states concerned.[12]

The principle of non- intervention

Art. 2 para 7 of the UN Charter prohibits the UN to intervene in matters which are essentially within the domestic jurisdiction of any state or to require from the member state to submit such matter to settlement. The only exception of non-intervention is the application of enforcement measures under Chapter VII. The scope of the conception of the matters essentially within domestic jurisdiction applies to all matters that are not regulated by international rules in principle, despite the fact that there might be some international treaty which such matter covers.[13] In the practice of the GA, there are numerous resolutions referring to the member states generally or particularly that would be considered the intervention to the domestic jurisdiction. The existence of customary rules which limited the scope of domestic jurisdiction can be then "justified" by the practice of the GA, but also by the reactions of member states to that practice. Thus, gross violations of human rights, or the process of de-colonisation are to be considered the matters where the UN acts or has acted without accusation of intervening in the domestic affairs.[14]

---

[11]Customary rule "pacta sunt servanda" restated by Art. 26 of the Vienna Convention on the Law of Treaties (1969),1155 UNTS 331 (22 May 1969).

[12] The scope of the principle covers *bona fide* effort of states to resort to one of the peaceful means (mediation, conciliation, negotiation, arbitration, submitting the dispute before the ICJ e.g.), the obligation to continue to seek peaceful settlement in a case of failure of one of the peaceful means and the obligation to abstain from *mala fide* actions which aggravate the situation already endangering the international peace or security. The UNGA Res 2625(XXV) (24 October 1970), the Declaration of Friendly Relations, restates the principle of peaceful settlement in para 3 and para 4 of Principle II.

[13]By international customary rules, the treatment of citizens, organization of government and use of state's territory are matters falling within the domestic jurisdiction of particular state.

[14] The UNGA Res. 53/164 (25 February 1999) condemned gross violation of human rights in Kosovo.

The principle of prohibition of threat or use of force

The principle has become fundamental, evolving its importance from the main purpose of the UN to maintain international peace and security, aiming not just against the use of force but the threat as well.[15] The statement of Dinstein "Nowdays, the prohibition of the use of inter-state force, as articulated in Ar. 2 para 4 of the Charter, has become an integral part of customary international law." stresses out the subjects protected by the principles who are not just members but non members as well.[16] Between the scholars the permissive and restrictive views of the prohibition of the force have developed. The restrictive view can be characterized by statement that "The use of force according to the Charter is permissible in two cases only: in the case of enforcement measures of the SC and of the implementation of the right of the individual or collective self-defence".[17] The practice of the states shows the tendency to justify unlawful actions of states not by invoking the mentioned exceptions of the principle but by the modification of the scope of the general rule of the prohibition. Such practice of states appears to be conformed with the permissive view of some scholars such as Amerasinghe who states "...the force, or the threat of it, by any individual or collectivity of states against the territorial integrity and political independence of any state which is consistent with the purposes of the UN is permitted.[18] However, such application appears to be controversial.[19]

---

[15] From the context of the UN Charter, a content of the term force as armed force has evolved. Measures short of armed force, like economic boycott, cannot be then considered the threat or use of the force. ICJ in its Advisory Opinion from 8.July 1996 on Legality of the threat or use of nuclear weapons in paragraph 47 states "The notions of "threat" or "use of force" under Article 2 para 4, of the Charter stand together in the sense that if the use of force itself in a given case is illegal, for whatever reason, the threat to use such force will likewise be illegal.", *Legality of the threat or use of nuclear weapons* (Advisory Opinion) [1996] ICJ >http://www.icj-cij.org/icjwww/icases/iunan/iunanframe.htm accessed on 2 November 2006.

[16] Yoram Dinstein, *War, aggression and self-defence* (fourth edition, Cambridge University Press, London 2005) 92.

[17] J.Mrazek, "Prohibition of the use and threat of force; Self-Defence and Self-Help in International Law" (1989) 27 CYIL 81-112.

[18] C.F.Amerasinghe, *Principles of the international law of international organizations* (second edition, Cambridge University Press, London 2005) 507-510.

[19] By applying such rule, the right of pre-emptive self-defence and the right to humanitarian intervention are covered by the international customary rule. But Art. 51 justifies the use of force in self-defence only when armed attack occurs. Thus, the argument of Amerasinghe that when the use of force is resorted in absence of an armed attack, the SC must use Art.39 and Art. 24, seems controversial. Under the mentioned provisions the member states confer to the SC the primary responsibility for the maintenance of the international peace and security and oblige themselves to abstain from the resorting to force in case when there is no armed attack (no legal justification for self-defence) and where is then under the determination of the SC to decide whether there are the prerequisites to resort to use force (existence of threat to the peace or breach of peace).If there are by the decision of the SC such prerequisites to use the force, the action has to be done under the supervision of the SC and with its control from the beginning as

Thus, again, one can argue that the use of force by states (as it can be seen in practice) can be considered the abrogation of Art.2 para 4 and possibly the non-existence of customary rule of the prohibition of the use of force. The advisory opinion of the ICJ in Nicaragua case in which the court doesn't consider that, for the rule to be established as customary rule, the corresponding practice must be in absolute conformity with the rule, appears to be an answer to that question, even though the ICJ did not state what the scope of such customary rule is.[20]

The principle of the obligation of the UN to ensure that non-members act in accordance with the principles of the UN Charter

The UN organs fulfill such obligation through exercising their power, by making the recommendations to non-member states as far as they are necessary for the maintaining the international peace and security. Bearing in mind the treaty character of the UN Charter and mandatory character of the recommendations, international customary law that treaty cannot bind third state is thus not violated. The question of such violation arises with the resolution of the SC under Chapter VII which has binding character. However, invoking Conforti "…the provisions of Chapter VII ,far from creating obligation for non-members states are provisions…in their favour.[21]

The principle of setting forth the obligation of member states to assistance in actions taking in accordance with the UN Charter and the obligation of member states to refrain from the assistance to states against which the UN takes enforcement or preventive measures.

The principle further restates the obligation of Art. 2 para 2 and details the duty of the member states to secure the success of the enforcement measures adopted by the SC in accordance with Chapter VII.

---

to limitate the ill-use of the force by member states.

[20]*Nicaragua case* (Merit) ICJ 1984 >http://www.icj-cij.org/icjwww/icases/inus/inus-ijudgment/inus-ijudhment-19860627.pdf accessed on 4 November 2006.

[21] Benedetto Conforti, *The law and practice of the United Nations,*(third revised edition, Martinus Njhoff Publishers, Boston 2005) 126-130.

The assessment of the principal organs of the UN.

The UN consists of these principal organs: the SC, the GA , the Secretariat, the Trusteeship Council, the International Court of Justice (hereinafter the ICJ), Economic and Social Council (hereinafter the ECOSOC).

The GA

The maintenance of international peace and security

The competence of the GA in maintaining the international peace and security has been set forth in a broad scope under Chapter IV of the UN Charter. Even without binding effect of the recommendation such power of the GA has an impact on the most important political and international issues. One of the most important functions appears the peaceful settlement function which the GA exercise under the Chapter VI in correlation with Chapter IV, and thus it can recommend to the party to dispute to resort to the one of the peaceful means of settlement of disputes, or to suggest the solution, or to establish the necessary subsidiary organ for the settlement.[22] The broad scope of the function of the GA in the maintaining the international peace and security is limited by Art. 2 para 7 (non-intervention in matters essentially within the domestic jurisdiction of particular state) and by Art. 12 (if the SC is exercising the functions of the maintenance of the international peace and security) which considering the ICJ advisory opinion has to be interpreted restrictively.[23] As it can be seen from the previous statement, the action of the GA under the Chapter VI is undisputable, there might be some tendency to justify the action of the GA under the Chapter VII of the UN Charter. The provision of the Art. 11, para 2 "…Any such question, on which action is necessary, shall be referred to the SC…", ensures the position of the GA to maintain international peace and security without resorting to enforcement measures under Chapter VII. Nevertheless, the GA has acted controversial on basis of the "Uniting for peace resolution" adopted in

---

[22] The UNGA Res. 40/188 (17 December 1985) calls the group of states to abolish the unilateral trade embargo against Nicaragua.

[23] The ICJ in its advisory opinion from July 9th, 2004 expressed that the GA by requesting the advisory opinion did not exceed its competence and thus did not violate Art.12 para 1, invoking the practice developed over the years when the GA acted in parallel with the SC, stressing out that while the SC has focused on matters concerning the maintenance of the international peace, the GA has dealt with the matters in broader view, mostly considering humanitarian or economic aspects; *The legal consequences of the construction the wall in the occupied Palestinians territories* (Advisory Opinion) ICJ 2004

1950 as consequence of the existence of paralyzed SC during the Cold War.[24] The resolution was referred to by the SC as foundation for transferring the question on Suez crisis (Israeli attack on Egypt) to the GA, which later has adopted the resolutions essential for the creation of the United Nations Emergency Force I.[25] The controversial issue was dealt within the ICJ later in its advisory opinion in a case Certain Expenses of the United Nations.[26] The ICJ in its advisory opinion did not consider the Uniting for Peace Resolution a legal basis for the GA to establish the UNEF I, instead, it did rule that the UNEF I has a character of peacekeeping operation adopted under Art. 14 of the UN Charter as opposed to enforcement measures of Chapter VII. The opinion on the Uniting for the Peace Resolution that "Resolution may now be treated as justifiable, at least to the extent that it envisages a peacekeeping operation as opposed to enforcement action on the basis of the purposes and principles of the organisation"[27] can be then implicitly derived from the advisory opinion of the ICJ. Despite the opinion of the ICJ the peacekeeping character of the UN forces and thus also UNEF I still remains controversial. The legitimity of UNEF I can be justified in that particular case only by the consent of all states concerned in Suez crisis and fact that it has acted as buffer between Egypt and Israel and has never resorted to force. However, the resolution itself cannot be the legal basis for the GA to adopt the enforcement measures, such competence belongs exclusively to the SC under Art. 42. Another controversial issue

---

>http://www.icj-cij.org/icjwww/idocket/imwp/timeframe.htm accessed on 29 October 2006.

[24] The GA has adopted the resolution 337/V in 1950 "Uniting for peace", allowing the GA to make appropriate recommendations to members for collective measures when the SC is paralysed in the process of dealing with the existence of the threat to the peace or breach of the peace or act of aggression, and made recommendation for members to have armed forces ready for purpose of the restoring the international peace and security. The resolution as such has allowed the GA to undertake the power of the SC to determine a threat to the peace, breach of the peace and take appropriate measures, including the use of force. The resolution was certainly the result of the existence of the Cold War and it was a basis for the GA to act when the SC is paralysed mostly because of the threat of the one or more of permanent members to use a right of veto; The UNGA Res. 337/V (3 November 1950).

[25] UNEF I. were set up by the Secretary General (res. no.998-ES I of November 4,1956, res. No 1000-ES I of November 5, 1956). The creation of UNEF I was denounce by some member states due to having the character of enforcement measure of Art. 42 of the UN Charter and resulted into the refusal of those states to participate in expenses covering the support of UNEF I. The member states which assented with the resolutions of the GA argued that UNEF I had no mean of the force, but right the opposite, it was a measure adopted under the Art. 14 of the UN Charter, as peaceful mean of the maintaining of international peace.

[26] The advisory opinion of the ICJ "Certain expenses of the UN" concerns the refusal of member states to participate in expenses covering the UNEF I based on its character of enforcement measure; *Certain expenses of the UN* (Advisory Opinion) ICJ 1962 >http://www.icj-cij.org/icjwww/idecisions/isummaries/iceunsummary620720.htm accessed on 2 November 2006.

[27] Philippe Sands and Pierre Klein, *Bowett's Law of International Institutions* (fifth edition, Sweet and Maxwell, London 2001) 35.

concerns the resolutions of the GA which recommend the sanctions short of the use of force.[28] The provision of Art. 41 entrusts the competence to decide on the enforcement measures short of armed force fundamentally to the SC, thus only non binding character of the resolutions of the GA in this case would be then the only legitimate justification for such action.

The other competence of the GA

The GA has not acted like legislative organ, its resolutions do not have normative character and do not bind the member states, but bearing in mind the consensus of the majority of states in the process of the adoption of the resolutions, the GA practice has the ability to show the development of the international customary rule.[29]

The SC

Maintenance of the international peace and security

Under Art. 24 the SC has a primary responsibility for the maintenance of international peace and security. Nonetheless the strong position of the SC in exercising the reconciliatory function under the Chapter VI., the outcome of the function is conditioned by the will of the parties to dispute.[30] The investigation of the situation which might lead to the dispute by the SC envisaged in Art.34 can constitute the foundation not only for the reconciliatory function under the Chapter VI but also for the function under the Chapter VII (enforcement measures).

Enforcement measures under the Chapter VII.

The provisions of the Chapter VII enable the SC after determination of the threat to the peace, breach of the peace, or act of aggression to recommend or to decide on

---

[28] The UNGA Res. 39/72 A (14 December 1984) on the economic sanctions of South Africa as consequence of the policy of the apartheid.

[29] The resolutions of the GA adopted under the treaty law (Covenant on Economic, Social, Cultural Rights and Covenant on Political and Civil Rights) and open for ratification of states have significant normative character because of their obligations towards states as parties to the treaties and they have to be distinguished from the resolutions of the GA adopted under the UN Charter; 999 UNTS 171 (23 March 1976).

[30] Except the general request (addressed to the states by the SC to settle the dispute by peaceful means), the SC can also make a recommendation, at any stage of dispute, of particular procedures and methods for adjustment with consideration of settling the dispute by submitting it for decision to the ICJ. Thus, the SC Res. 1947, recommended Great Britain and Albania to submit the dispute of the Corfu Channel for decision to the ICJ; The UNSC Res. (22 April 1947).

enforcement measures. Art. 40 covers the provisional measures which main character is to prevent the worsening of the situation and in the practice they might be accompanied by enforcement measures.[31] The SC can resort to enforcement measures not involving the use of armed force[32] or to adopt the enforcement measures involving the use of armed force against the responsible state.[33] In both cases the exception of Art. 2 para 7 doesn't apply which allows the SC to act even in domestic crisis. The ineffectiveness of the UN forces[34] resulted in the SC practice to authorise the member states in executing the military operations either individually or within the regional organisations.[35] Despite the clear authorisation of regional organisation covered by Art.53, the authorisation of member states to resort to force appears controversial.[36]

---

[31]The SC resolution 1199 of September 23 1998, concerns the civil war in Kosovo, includes the provisional measure on cease-fire together with the sanctions under Art. 41; The UNSC Res. 1199 (23 September 1947).

[32] Such measures are inter alia partial or complete interruption of economic relations, and air, rail, sea and other means of communication. The SC resolution from 1992 obligated the member states to adopt the economic sanctions including embargo on imports and exports, the blocking of financial operations, against the Republic of Yugoslavia; The UNSC Res. 757 (30 May 1992).

[33] The SC has acted under Art. 42 directly using the armed groups of the member states under the international command with the supervision of the SC (UNPROFOR in former Yugoslavia or ONUSOM in Somalia).

[34] Such failure was represented in Somalia. The UN force ONUSOM I in Somalia was established in 1992 as peacekeeping operation with the main purpose of humanitarian assistance but consequently with the deteriorating the situation by the SC Resolution 837/1993 it has changed to peace-enforcing character of ONUSOM II which has resulted into the killing of innocent victims and subsequent withdrawal of the UN force; The UNSC Res 837/1993 (6 June 1993).

[35] Art. 53 enables the SC to authorise the regional organisation to resort to force, even though the SC has never done that it has on numerous cases authorised the regional organisation to use force (e.g. in 1993 after three months of unauthorised action of NATO in Kosovo, the SC by resol. 1244/1999 established the interim administration involving also NATO forces -KFOR); such post-authorisation of use of force cannot legally justified the action of NATO, the only justification of legitimity of NATO actions would be here the application of moral rules regarding the gross violation of human rights.

[36] In 1950 the SC has authorised the member states to help South Korea against North Korea and in 1991 the member states where authorised to help Kuwait to return its territory occupied by Iraq. The authorisation of the SC which came from the resolution of SC in 1991 against Iraq seems to be superfluous because of the fact that member states has acted in collective self-defence under Art. 51 for which the authorisation is not needed. Because of the fact that the UN Charter doesn't expressly enable the SC to authorise the member states to resort to force individually the explicitness of the authorisation seems to be essential. Thus, implicit authorisation invoked by the coalition states in the case of occupation of Iraq in 2003 cannot be the justification for the states to resort to force; even post-authorisation of the SC (which occurred after the invasion of Iraq by coalition states) cannot justified the unauthorised action because of the necessity to control such action from the beginning by the SC which has the primary responsibility in maintaining the international peace and security; The UNSC Res. 678 (29 November 1991).

The ICJ

Contentious jurisdiction

The ICJ is principal judicial organ of the UN[37] consisted of judges not representing their states but acting in their professional capacity. The ICJ exercises its facultative contentious jurisdiction over the states as parties to dispute at states' instance, the member states thus do not have an obligation to submit the dispute to the ICJ for the decision.[38] The negative elements of contentious jurisdiction of the ICJ are the non-existence of the appeal system and the lack of the effectiveness of the enforcement measures to comply with the judgment.[39]

Advisory opinion of the ICJ

The ICJ exercises its advisory opinion function in accordance with the UN Charter.[40] Despite the non-binding character of the advisory opinion, the ICJ has declared in many cases *opinio juris necessitates* which together with the practice of the states have confirmed the existence of the international customary rule.[41] The ICJ's advisory function can sometimes concern the legal question which might fall within the subject of the dispute between the states, thus it is on the ICJ's discretion to decide whether to give the advisory opinion or not and thus whether the lack of consent of the state concerned is relevant or not.[42] Not just because of non binding character of advisory

---

[37] Art. 92 of the UN Charter.

[38] The member states thus do not have the obligation to resort to the ICJ as one of the mean of peaceful settlement. The obligatory jurisdiction of the ICJ can arise from the unilateral optional clause under the condition of reciprocity of the counterpart, by the agreement of states to submit *ad hoc* dispute to the ICJ, or by the optional clause on obligatory jurisdiction of the ICJ in the agreements between states on disputes *pro futuro* arising from that agreement.

[39] Even though Art. 94 (2) gives the SC the power to undertake the measures to give effect to the decision of the ICJ when state fails to comply with the judgment, in practice the SC has never acted this way. The effectiveness of the enforcement measure becomes more doubtful in the case when one of the permanent members of the SC is state who fails to comply with the judgment (veto power).

[40] The ICJ gives the advisory opinion on the request of the GA or the SC on any legal question (Art.96 para 1), and on request of other organs of the UN or specialized agencies under the condition of the authorisation of the GA to do so and only within the scope of their activities (Art.96 para 2). Thus in 1993 the ICJ refused to give an advisory opinion on legality of the use of nuclear weapons by States on base that such question falls out of the scope of the Health World Organization which requested the advisory opinion even though that the GA gave the HWO the general authorisation to request the advisory opinion, *Legality of the use by a state of nuclear weapons in armed conflict* (Advisory opinion) 1996, http://www.icj-cij.org/icjwww/icases/iahw/ianframe.htm accessed on 2 November 2006.

[41] The Advisory opinion of the ICJ of 29 of May 1951 regarding the making the reservations to the Convention on Genocide has had a significant effect on the customary international law, *Reservations to the Convention on the Prevention and Punishment of the Crime of Genocide* (Advisory Opinion) ICJ 1950 >http://www.icj-cij.org/icjwww/icases/iahw/ianwframe.htm accessed on 29 October 2006.

[42] The ICJ has confirmed the admissibility of the request of the GA of the Advisory opinion concerning

opinion but also because of necessity to ensure the co-operation between the UN organs the advisory function of the ICJ shouldn't be conditioned to the consent of the states concerned in matters.[43]

The ECOSOC

The main task of the ECOSOC is to promote the international cooperation in social and economic field.[44]

The Secretariat

The Secretariat comprises from the Secretary-General and the staff carrying out executive functions of the organisation.[45]

The Trusteeship Council

The function of the Trusteeship Council is due to the independence of Palau, as last trusteeship territory, is 1994 suspended.[46]

---

the construction of the wall in occupied territory of Palestine; the ICJ in its advisory opinion (Advisory opinion) of July 9-th of 2004 para. 49 declared that the subject-matter of the request for the advisory opinion is not a bilateral matter between Israel and Palestine but concern of the UN in relations to the international peace and security, *Legal consequences of the construction of a wall in occupied Palestinian territory* (Advisory Opinion) ICJ 2004 >http://www.icj-cij.org/icjwww/idocekt/imwp/imframe.htm accessed on 29 October 2006.

[43] Thus, in cases where the parties to dispute do not seek the settlement through the jurisdiction of the ICJ, the advisory function seems to be the one of the effective means to endorse the functioning and co-operation of the organs of the UN in maintaining the international peace and security.

[44] The effectiveness of the function of the ECOSOC is given by the co-operation with the other bodies of the UN. Thus, the ECOSOC prepares the studies in general or specific and makes recommendation to the GA, members of the UN or specialised agencies. The one of the main scope of the function towards the GA is preparing the draft conventions for submission to the GA (e.g. Convention on Genocide). Within the council there are numerous functional commissions established by subject-matter (on human rights, on narcotic drugs, etc.) and 5 regional commissions for 1.Europe, 2.Asia, 3.Latin America and the Carribean,4.Africa and 5.Western Asia.

[45] The Secretary-General is chief administrative officer of the UN but he also participates in the function of the maintaining the international peace and security e.g. the UN SG acts as mediators or offers good offices in peaceful settlement. Such function doesn't derive explicitly from the UN Charter but is given by his moral and political authority and is proven to be useful.

[46] The Trusteeship Council had exercised its function in the scope of being the organ of supervision over the trusteeship territories after the de-colonisation.

Conclusion

Despite the success of the UN in the field of de-colonisation, protection of environment, or development of international law, less successful performance in the scope of the maintaining of international peace and security is obvious. But one has to be mindful of the position of the UN as possessing the legal personality but consisting of sovereign states which sometimes less and sometimes more passionate pursue their own interests, most of the time justifying their actions by their own application of the provisions of the UN Charter. Thus, nowadays in the time of the global threat of using nuclear weapons or terrorism, the position of the UN in ensuring the international peace and security is conditioned by the awareness of states of such position and by the submission of their own interests to the maintaining the international peace and security of international community as whole.[47]

---

[47] The amendment of the UN Charter would be the one of possible tools to update or to detail some of the provisions and to make them conformed with the recent development of the situation in world but taking into account the provision of Art. 108 such decision would require ratification not only qualified majority of the GA but affirmative vote of all permanent members which seems almost unattainable.

Bibliography

Amerasinghe C. F., *Principles of the international law of international organizations* (second edition, Cambridge University Press, London 2005).

Brownlie I., *Principles of Public International Law* ,(sixth edition Oxford University Press Oxford 2003).

Cassese A., *International Law,* (second edition, Oxford University Press, 2005).

Conforti B., *The law and practice of the United Nations,*(third revised edition, Martinus Njhoff Publishers, Boston 2005).

Dinstein Yoram, *War, aggression and self-defence* (fourth edition, Cambridge University Press, London 2005).

Sands P. and Klein P., *Bowett' s Law of International Institutions* (fifth edition, Sweet and Maxwell, London 2001).

Simma B., *The Charter of the UN - a commentary* (second edition, Oxford University Press, Oxford 2005).

Journal

T. Franck, "Who killed Art.2 (4)" or changing norms governing the use of force by states" (1970) 64 AJIL 809-837.

J. Mrazek, "Prohibition of the use and threat of force; Self-Defence and Self-Help in International Law" (1989) 27 CYIL 81-112.

Cases

Corfu Channel Case (UK v .Albania) (Merits) [1949] ICJ

Nicaragua case (Merit) ICJ 1984

Web site

www.un.org